365 Connecting Questions for Couples

One Conversation a Day for a Journey into Love to Grow a Powerful Relationship.

GARY LOVE

Table of Contents

INTRODUCTION

The most crucial aspect that you should know about communication is that it goes deeper than words. There are four main types of communication that people use to transmit information: verbal (which uses speaking or sign language), nonverbal (body language, expressions, gestures), written (via texts, e-mails, letters, symbols such as emojis) and visual (through art, photographs, and charts).

Depending on a person's character, personality type, and upbringing, they express themselves in different ways. An outspoken individual will be very open about verbally declaring his/her feelings. In contrast, an individual who grew up in a strict family might be more likely to show off their feelings through nice gestures and actions. Similarly, artists who are usually introverts that lack social skills will prefer to express themselves through their work or in an indirect manner (via text, email) rather than face-to-face. Part of being a couple is understanding how your partner expresses their love and accepting it for what it is, rather than forcing them to express themselves differently. For example, someone who is very outspoken may want or expect their partner to be like that too, despite their preference to show love through kind gestures.

It is not easy to be an effective communicator because it is not always apparent what your partner wants or what they are saying. However, it is way too easy to assume that you got the memo, and by doing that, unknowingly misinterpret what has been said. Communication is something that requires a lot of trial and error, and plenty of reassurance. Issues that remain unsolved never go away and should be properly discussed whenever you and your partner feel ready to have a conversation. Keep in mind that, when you are in a relationship, there are two sides to every situation/issue/problem, and to reach an agreement, both sides need to be understood and analyzed.

Honesty plays a significant role in the communication game. If you cannot be honest about your feelings, you cannot expect your partner to understand you and act accordingly either. Having an open mind is also crucial to become a better communicator. A person with an open mind is more likely to try and get an explanation before coming to their conclusion in any event or circumstance. They will consider the likelihood that they might be wrong. Another key element of improving the way you communicate is the willingness to take charge and directly ask for your partner's perspective. Sometimes we need to let go of our egos and take the first step. There is no shame in asking, "How are you feeling?" or "How can I help you?" and there is surely no shame in being the first to say, "I'm sorry," "I was wrong," or admitting that you did not understand what they were trying to say.

Similarly, the
Question: "Do you want to know what I want?" serves as a very powerful tool that aids in shifting someone's focus from their point of view toward your perspective. It gives you the chance to compare both sides of the story. In a matter of seconds, the conversation can go from confrontational to an open discussion.

Constructive communication requires two people who care about each other and are willing to do whatever it takes to effectively deliver their message and be receptive to their partner's message. Remember to be kind, patient, non-judgmental, and have an open mind. The results are worth it.

Before we dive right into this book, I have something to ask of you. Have an open mind and do not judge your partner. Whether you treat this as a game or as a serious conversation starter, there should be no fear of "wrong answers." Even if your partner offers up an answer you do not agree with, it does not invalidate the answer itself. There is no wrong response. Rather than judging your partner for their answers that you don't agree with, try conversing with them and assessing why he/she feels/thinks that way, and only after you understand their reasoning explain your take on it.

Intimacy in relationships can be defined as a feeling of being connected to someone on an emotional, physical, and mental level. You can be intimate with a whole bunch of people, in the sense that you feel comfortable talking to them about anything and sharing your deepest feelings. Intimacy in a romantic relationship still focuses on this feeling of closeness, while also having the added physical aspect to it, which more often than not, complicates things. A healthy and intimate relationship makes us feel accepted and loved. It allows us to be vulnerable and express ourselves freely, without the fear of being judged or criticized. Many people are under the false impression that a healthy intimate life means having good sexual experiences. Still, our sex life is usually influenced by how emotionally intimate we are with our partners. A couple who has many different ways of expressing love and affection will have a more fulfilling sexual life, regardless of how 'spicy' or 'kinky' the physical representation of their love is.

According to Sheri Stritof, the ingredients you need in

order to have a healthy sex life are love, acceptance, the ability to have meaningful conversations, the will to make time for each other, having fun/being playful, and physical attraction. In other words, if you want a fulfilling sexual life, first you need to have a genuine connection with your partner (we are talking about couples who want to spend their whole lives with each other, not just a few weeks or months of sexual gratification).

Creating a real sense of intimacy is hard. One major reason is that it relies so much on how you communicate with your partner. If you feel like your lover does not understand you or your needs, it's hard to feel connected with each other. However, if you have trouble with being open about your needs and expectations, then realize that your partner is not a mind reader. To feel a sense of connection with each other, both partners need to express themselves and be mindful of each other openly. Small yet pivotal improvements in communication alone make a big difference in the level of intimacy between you and your partner.

CHAPTER ONE
HOW TO USE THIS BOOK

If you are reading this book alone, I strongly suggest you involve your partner and read the book together from the beginning. Make this a project the two of you undertake as a team. You both want to enter this work with the specific intention of strengthening and protecting your relationship, in addition to building intimacy and learning more about each other. These questions can be fun, humorous, enlightening, and deeply moving. You will be surprised at how much more you discover about yourself and about each other.

You also will be challenged to make some personal changes in your behaviors, habits, and words. The questions will reveal unmet needs and behavior change requests from both of you. You will want to discuss these needs and requests and what you are each willing to change or accommodate for the other. There might be needs you cannot fulfill or changes you're unwilling to make, and this will require honest and open discussion, so you can mutually arrive at alternative solutions.

There are 365 questions in the book. Consider working through the questions every day. Both of you should keep a journal to make notes about your partner's responses and your own feelings after you complete the questions. You will also want to write down specific action steps both of you will take if a question prompts an adjustment in attitude, behavior, communication, or values.

When you begin a topic, you will each ask and answer the same question, taking turns as the first person to answer a question. It is often more challenging to be the first one to answer, as you might need time for your true feelings to bubble to the surface—or you might feel reticent to be fully open in your response. Also, your partner's answers can influence your responses, so be mindful that your answers reflect your own true feelings and needs.

Your partner's answers or your own reactions might stimulate more questions or conversation between you, which can further develop connection and intimacy. Just be sure you listen intently to your partner's responses without interrupting or getting distracted. Sit close together as you are asking and answering, holding hands, or touching. Even if your partner's answer makes you bristle or feel uncomfortable, try hard to listen without anger or judgment merely. Invite your partner to dig deeper and share more by asking, “Is there more?” once he or she answers the question. Keep asking this until your partner has nothing left to add.

Should any of your discussions about these questions become too emotional or trying to sort through without pain and anger, please seek the support of a strained relationship counselor to help you navigate the issue. Sometimes old wounds and pain from the past are too entrenched to unravel and heal without the help of a therapist. If this is the case, do not allow this emotional division to languish between you. Put your relationship first by seeking to treat and heal any fissures that could ultimately pull you apart or undermine the happiness of your connection.

Find a room in your home that feels peaceful and uncluttered without potential distractions or interruptions. Allow yourself an hour to finish all ten questions from one section and to discuss your feelings and reactions. Inform anyone else who lives in the house not to interrupt you during this hour. If necessary, leave the house to go to a quiet restaurant, sit somewhere in nature, or park the car somewhere in a peaceful setting. Consider this sacred time together that not only contributes to your happiness as a couple but also makes you better parents, friends, and professionals. Your relationship happiness is the linchpin for happiness in all other areas of your life.

So, are you ready to get started?

Here are a few reminders:

- Grab your journals and get a glass of water or a cup of tea (try to avoid alcohol as it alters your verbal self-control).
- Find your peaceful spot in the house or elsewhere.
- Flip a coin to see who will be the first one to answer the first question. Then alternate after that. Read the question and the information below the question out loud. Then ask the question again directly to your partner.
- Try not to read ahead to the next questions, but instead focus intently on the question you are asking and answering.
- Sit close to each other so you can touch and look at each other face to face.
- Give each other plenty of time to respond, and as you are listening to your partner to answer a question, try not to think ahead about your own answers. Just be fully present for your partner and practice empathic listening skills.

If your partner reveals a request for

a change from you, discuss and write down specific actions steps you both intend to take and when you intend to take them. Making these changes can take time, as we need repetition and reinforcement to solidify new behaviors. Set up a system of gentle reminders and accountability for each other and be patient as you both strive to be a better, more attentive, loving partner for the other.

THIS IS OUR JOURNAL

(Put your name into the heart)

CHAPTER TWO
365 QUESTIONS FOR MARRIED COUPLES

Conversation Idea: Children have no limits in their thinking. Therefore, this is a great starting point for figuring out if you've both maintained (or evolved) your passions to date.

Question: As children, what did both of you want to be when you grew up?

Conversation Idea: Learning something together can strengthen your bond as a couple. If given a chance, what language would you like to learn and why are you interested in it?

Question: Are you interested in learning a foreign language?

Conversation Idea: Perhaps, you will discover something new about each other by discussing the things you really fancy doing since you were a little kid. Was there a particular skill you wish you had? With enough support from your partner, are you still willing to try it?

Question: Is there anything you would like to learn since you were a child?

Conversation Idea: Celebrating special events with your partner allows you to make more memories as a couple. On what particular occasion do you spend more time together and why is it important?

Question: What is one special occasion that you want to celebrate together?

Conversation Idea: An exciting relationship is something that encourages you to face your fears rather than succumb to them. What is one thing that you wish to try, individually or together, granting that you have enough courage to do so?

Question: If fear is not an obstacle, what challenges

are you willing to go through?

Conversation Idea: As much as we would like to be completely honest with our partners, we sometimes feel judged even before opening up to them. What is one thing you wish your partner could change in order for you to be more comfortable in sharing what you really feel?

Question: What usually hinders you from being fully open to someone?

Conversation Idea: As years pass by, you face different trials as a couple and, with enough love and trust, overcome them together. What particular life lesson do you think your future grandchildren should learn about?

Question: What life lesson would you probably tell your grandchildren in the future?

Conversation Idea: Some couples are not comfortable having this kind of conversation, particularly when they are in the early stage of their relationship. But if the time is finally right, what kind of family do you wish to build? Would you like just a small one, or do you believe that more is actually merrier?

Question: How many kids would you like to have?

Conversation Idea: Working on your future together is definitely good. Nevertheless, you have to take some time off to relax and refresh your whole being. What kind of activities would you like to do to reinvigorate yourself?

Question: If you have an entire week to spend on vacation, how exactly would you like to spend it?

Conversation Idea: Comparing each one's achievement, unfortunately, really happens during get-togethers. It makes a lot of people uncomfortable, particularly those who had it rough. What are the things you have accomplished as a couple that you would willingly share?

Question: In a class reunion, what are the things that you will openly share?

Conversation Idea: We all have our fair share of bad decisions, and some of these haunt us for a long time. What will you change if you ever get the chance?

Question: If you have the power to do things over again, what will you change in your life?

Conversation Idea: We all have that (childhood) hero in the form of our grandmother, favorite teacher, or best friend. Tell us more about this person. What did this person do for you to look up to him/her?

Question: Who do you consider your life hero?

Conversation Idea: Maintaining productivity and possibly stepping up the career ladder is no easy feat. You cheer each other up and find reasons to carry on. When the other one is getting burned out, what do you do to uplift his/her spirit?

Question: How do you motivate each other to persevere at work?

Conversation Idea: Whether or not you are in a relationship, it is always good to consider other people's feelings, especially if you are about to drop a sensitive comment. How do you handle insensitive actions? Do you usually keep it to yourself, or do you let the other person know about it?

Question: What, for you, is the most insensitive thing a person can do that may hurt your feelings?

Conversation Idea: We get to learn valuable life lessons from family and friends, but sometimes, we meet "temporary people" who share with us their inspiring or thought-provoking experiences. What are the 5 life-relevant lessons have you acquired from these people that you find true or useful?

Question: List down 5 important things in life that you have learned from random people.

Conversation Idea: Being a skillful person helps us accomplish a lot of things and may even be a reason for younger people to land a good job in the future.

Question: What are the 5 useful skills you wish to

acquire and why do you think they are relevant to your life?

Conversation Idea: Some people choose practicality over comfort, while some are willing to take their time in finding the job that would best suit their personality. Try to expand as to why you are not willing to take this particular job despite the good salary offer.

Question: What job would you never do no matter how good the pay is?

Conversation Idea: When our phobia is triggered by natural circumstances, it could hinder us from enjoying a lot of adventurous activities. Are your actions limited by certain phobias? How does it affect your life in general? Do you try to overcome this fear, or you just learned to live with it?

Question: Do you have any severe phobia?

Conversation Idea: Your partner may be thankful for your good traits, but there is someone else responsible for that; someone who has made a great impact in your life and later became a great influence in everything you do. Who is that person and in what way did he/she change your perspectives?

Question: Who has the greatest influence on your life?

Conversation Idea: Relationship means teamwork; it becomes more successful when the two people involved always have each other's back. In what way do you support one another?

Question: Write down 3 to 5 ways you support each other.

Conversation Idea: We all try to impress other people for many reasons, and it is actually a good thing because it could mean we are working hard to get what we want. But how far are you willing to go just to get someone's respect and admiration?

Question: How far would you go just to impress others?

Conversation Idea: Being confident helps us get through a lot of trials, be it at work or personal endeavors. What do you do in order to acquire enough assertiveness?

Question: How do you boost your self-confidence?

Conversation Idea: Every relationship is special, but what do you think makes your relationship unique? Is it the way you fix problems, or the way you communicate with each other?

Question: What makes your relationship unique?

Conversation Idea: Arguments and misunderstandings are part of any relationship; you just have to be respectful of your partner's decision and be considerate enough not to say hurtful things when both of your emotions are still high. What was the biggest fight you ever had?

Question: What was your biggest fight?

Conversation Idea: Jealousy is healthy, granting that you sit and discuss it, rather than succumb to your negative emotions. Are you the jealous type of partner? How do you deal with that feeling?

Question: What is your take on jealousy?

Conversation Idea: Comparisons are not always negative; if done carefully, it could actually help you work on your shortcomings. But what is your take on this? Do you sometimes compare yourself and feel insecure, or discover things you want to change?

Question: Do you ever compare yourself with others?

Conversation Idea: They say the sense of excitement fades away as soon as you get too comfortable with each other. But it does not apply to everyone. Keeping a relationship is a continuous process; you have to work on it on a daily basis to keep the spark alive. What do you do in order to put a little more excitement in your relationship?

Question: What makes a relationship exciting?

Conversation Idea: Sometimes, we prefer to keep our emotions to ourselves just to avoid misunderstandings and confrontations. But take this chance to finally get it off your chest – this could be a good time to discuss it with your partner and hopefully find a way to settle things out.

Question: Is there something you have been holding inside you that you want to let go?

Conversation Idea: This is just for fun: Have you ever had a stroke of luck and won something by chance? Some people even believe in lucky charms. Tell us about that time when you felt so lucky.

Question: Was there a time when you felt fortunate?

Conversation Idea: The need to conform to what the society generally believes to be right or acceptable could be really stressful. Have you ever felt that kind of pressure? How do you/would you handle this?

Question: Has the society ever put pressure on you?

Conversation Idea: Bad habits come in different forms: It could be in a form of vices like smoking and too much drinking or behavioral issues like procrastination. Either way, they could delay your personal progress and affect your life for the long haul. What bad habit/s do you want to break and how do you plan to do it?

Question: Any lousy habit you want to break?

Conversation Idea: Technology definitely makes our lives easier. But was there a time when you felt like it is becoming more of a problem that affects relationships? If so, in what way?

Question: How does technology affect personal relationships?

Conversation Idea: As we grow older and become more mature, we tend to lose interest in things we used to have fun doing, like playing video games, for example. Have this ever happened to you, or do you feel like you are actually starting to feel this way?

Question: Have you [recently] lost interest in something you used to enjoy?

Conversation Idea: Arguments are inevitable, but there is nothing good communication cannot resolve. Do you remember the reason behind this misunderstanding? How did you resolve it? What lessons have you learned after patching things up?

Question: When was the last time you argued with someone (not necessarily your partner)?

Conversation Idea: Not everyone gets to accomplish their goals on time. Many of us get stuck and go through an enormous amount of trials before being successful. What about you?

Question: Is there anything you wish you had accomplished earlier in life?

Conversation Idea: Admit it or not, most of us go through that phase where we are willing to go beyond our limitations just to prove how much we love someone. What is your story?

Question: What is the craziest, or perhaps the worst thing you did for love?

Conversation Idea: People are inclined to stick to a job they do not necessarily love just because it is practical to do so. Are you willing to give it up in order to acquire happiness and satisfaction, despite not being sure what the future holds?

Question: Are you willing to give up a really stable job in exchange for happiness?

Conversation Idea: They say we all deserve a second chance, but what are the factors you need to consider before deciding whether or not you should give someone that chance.

Question: When do you think someone deserves a second chance?

Conversation Idea: You can express your love in many different ways, but do you think you are expressive enough to let your partner know how much you appreciate him/her every day?

Question: Do you think you are able to express your love on a daily basis?

Conversation Idea: Sometimes, we need to sacrifice things or tolerate unwanted circumstances just to be with the person we love. What have you done to prove that you are serious about your relationship?

Question: In what way do you think you have proven your love to your partner?

Conversation Idea: Choosing the first present during the early stage of your relationship can be quite stressful, mainly because you are still trying to figure out what he/she likes and not. Share with us how you come up with that first present and how did your partner react to it.

Question: Tell us the story behind your first gift.

Conversation Idea: Men are probably not very comfortable with this question, but let us admit, love can make us go crazy. You are going to cry when it hurts, no matter how big or masculine you are. What was the mushiest thing you did just to make your partner happy?

Question: What was the most romantic thing you did for the sake of love?

Conversation Idea: Every time we commit mistakes, we also take away a portion of our partner's trust. If you do not take immediate action, this could damage the relationship in the future. What can you do in order to regain his/her lost trust?

Question: What can you do to regain your partner's trust?

Conversation Idea: For instance, we may feel uncomfortable around someone who is touchy-feely, so you ask your partner to set a certain distance whenever this person is around.

Question: Have you ever asked your partner to avoid certain people?

Conversation Idea: Without putting your personal situation in the picture, why do you think some people cheat? Is it a behavioral problem or the partner's effort is not really enough to make the other one satisfied?

Question: Why do others cheat?

Conversation Idea: Let us reminisce: What was the first thing that attracted you most about your partner during your first few meetings? Does he/she still carry the same personality?

Question: What did you first notice when you saw your partner for the first time?

Conversation Idea: Write down two things: Your partner's best and worst qualities. Explain your reasons for your answer. Again, be cool about it and you will be surprised at how positively it will affect your relationship.

Question: What are your partner's best and worst qualities?

Conversation Idea: Spending time with your partner is necessary for making your relationship strong. Instead of assuming that you are doing something great and then moving on, it is important to find out whether your partner appreciates your effort. This question helps partners understand their input into the relationship. In addition, it helps them understand whether they appreciate one another. If one or both partners do not appreciate each other's efforts, it means they must work hard at their relationship before the cracks become much bigger and lead to the death of the relationship. Spending time with your partner is something you simply cannot run from.

Question: Do you appreciate your partner's efforts to spend time with you?

Conversation Idea: It is necessary for partners to spend quality time together. By spending quality time together, they are in a position to understand each other even better. It does not matter how well two partners understand each other, but when they fail to spend significant time with one another, this opens up cracks in their relationship. Thus, asking this question helps determine whether both partners are happy with the amount of time they spend with one another. If they are not spending enough time with one another, they are certainly bound to become resentful of each other.

Question: Are you spending enough time with your partner?

Conversation Idea: At the end of the day, money runs the world. If you have money, you have power. It is important that partners understand what beliefs they each hold about money. If someone thinks that money is more important than their partner that the relationship cannot flourish. For a relationship to become successful, partners should consider each other as the prize, and that money cannot possibly take that away. Money is important, but it is certainly not the only thing. People should always concentrate on having great lives.

Question: Is money more important than your partner?

Conversation Idea: If a couple is not careful, they could easily find themselves doing things they would regret much later. And considering that human beings are not flawless, partners are bound to make various bad decisions. It is important that partners ask one another the various things they regret. This is not aimed at ruining their mood, but it gives them direction for, in the future, they know how they must act and behave in order to avoid further heartache. In the same breath, partners must be careful to ensure they are not bogged down by their past poor decisions, but rather they gain inspiration to act in a much better way.

Question: Do you regret anything?

Conversation Idea: Again, when we talk about taking kids to schools, we cannot fail to consider the schools that we would want our kids to attend. When partners are making this decision, it should not be lost on them that they can only wish because when it comes to joining certain schools, there are various expectations, and unless your kid has fulfilled these expectations, then they would not gain admission. By helping your kids gain an education from prestigious schools, you have done a lot in helping them get started on the right path to success.

Question: Which schools would you want your child to attend?

Conversation Idea: Another thing that parents must not forget is that their kid's talents can be a major force. When you look at most successful artists or athletes, you will realize that they began at a small age, which means they had been supported by their parents. In order to be truly amazing at the global stage, someone must start sharpening their talent from a young age. Thus, it is important that parents encourage their children and also support them in sharpening their talents and reaching for the stars. This will help them in becoming the best.

Question: Are you more into developing talents or academics?

Conversation Idea: It is also important that parents deliberate on how they will reward success. If a kid performs well and they are given a reward, it motivates them to keep a good performance, and it helps them to become great at what they are doing. But if a kid does well, and no one bothers to appreciate them, they will take to it in a bad attitude, and this could discourage them from being more hard-working, which could easily set them on the path of being underachievers. Thus, it is important that parents deliberate on how they are going to reward their kids. Also, it is important to note that the best rewards are not necessarily the most expensive, but they need to be well thought out.

Question: How do you reward success?

Conversation Idea: Kids are pretty impressionable. Sadly, this means they can adapt bad behaviors pretty quickly. This is something that all parents should expect. But when it happens, it is important to know how to discipline them, in order to deter them from repeating their bad habits, behaviors and encourage them to be well-behaved. This conversation helps parents determine their way of disciplining their kids. When you have disciplined kids, that is a huge achievement, for it empowers them to develop the mindset of winners.

Question: What is your preferred style of discipline?

Conversation Idea: Parents must be aware of the fact that school at present is a bit different from what school used to be years ago. Nowadays, there are so many negative influences that make it hard for kids to become straightened easily. It is the duty of the parent to understand the various things that make it hard to discipline a kid and to help them get started on the right path. But then again, taking notice of these unhealthy practices in schools is not enough, but parents must be willing to think creatively in order to find how to navigate through these issues.

Question: What is the worst thing about school today?

Conversation Idea: For the longest time, it used to be, go to school, get good grades, get a good job, earn a great salary, and become successful. To an extent, this is how things still operate. But then the world has become more accommodative to other formulas of success. Today, you may find a kid opening a YouTube channel, and within a year, they will be making more money than a successful CEO. So, this begs the Question; is book smarts the only ticket to success? Of course, the answer is no! But this is not to mean that you shouldn't take your kids to school, but rather, you should take them to school until they are mature enough to know what they want out of life.

Question: Do you consider book smarts the ticket to success?

Conversation Idea: Considering that there are so many avenues toward success in the modern world, it is not a must that you child reaches the highest level of education, but then it helps that your child has some form of education, because apart from gaining technical skills, and education helps someone know how to live with people. Thus, parents should have this conversation touching on what level of education they wish their kids to achieve.

Question: What education level do you wish your child to reach?

Conversation Idea: Education is important, there is no doubt about that, but then one must be aware about the fact that their child could fail in school. So, when this happens, how do they move on? First off, it is important to understand the reasons behind their child failing in school. If the kid has a high IQ but somehow was not serious, they could always give it another go. If the kid is demonstrably disinterested in school but have a passion for other things, they should support the kid in what they are passionate about.
Question: What would you do if your kid failed in school?

Conversation Idea: Parents must also discuss what would make them proud parents. Obviously, every parent would consider themselves successful if their kids accomplished their important goals, but then, there are other metrics to measure success as a parent. For instance, some parents might consider themselves successful if they have raised kids who are self-confident, and who have great social skills. Some parents might consider themselves successful when they have raised kids who are appreciative of their effort, who pursue their talents, and who are hard-working. It is important for parents to hold this discussion because it helps them to determine whether they have been successful at raising a great family, or they have failed.

Question: What is your idea of success as a parent?

Conversation Idea: This question could be answered differently by various parents. Some parents think that it is not okay to love one child more than the rest, but other parents think that it is totally okay to love one child over the rest. For a child to become the favorite of their parent, they must stand out in certain regard, or they must be more resourceful than the rest. Whether this is a good or bad thing is a subjective matter. But at the end of the day, the fact remains that some parents have favorite kids.

Question: Do you have a favorite kid?

Conversation Idea: Handling kids is not an easy job. When you go on outings, you might expect that kids will be hard to handle, especially when they are still young. During such moments, you feel provoked, and you certainly must act. Do you keep silent on their behavior and make a mental note to talk with your kids once you go back, or do you shame them in public? It is important that you realize that public shaming does not always work as you hoped. In some instances, public shaming can hurt a kid's self-esteem, and also cause them to resent their parent, which makes it difficult to have a good relationship with your kid.

Question: What is your take on public shaming your kids?

Conversation Idea: For day 64–73: There is a point you get in a relationship, and you begin to wonder if everything is going well. Am I doing the right thing? Is she happy with me? Am I enough for him? If these little sparks of wonder go unanswered, worry and anxiety will set in, and that is never a good thing. The best course of action will be to voice these thoughts to your partner and put those concerns to bed. Here are some romantic questions to ask your partner to keep things exciting and intimate and, at the same time, provide some much-needed assurance.

Question: What is your favorite memory of our time together?

Question: What do you think is my best physical feature?

Question: When do you feel the most protected and loved around me?

Question: What do I do that you wish I would do more often?

Question: When did you first feel I was very attractive?

Question: Do you like my kisses or hugs more?

Question: What is your wildest fantasy?

Question: What do you think makes me smile the most?

Question: What do I do that turns you on the most?

Question: What is the most romantic thing I've ever done for you?

Conversation Idea: For day 74-84: Rome was not built in a day. Relationships take time and effort, and the work process of that is usually imperfect and stressful, but the results, in the end, make every move worth it. It is essential to take some time to get up close and personal with your partner, achieving new levels of intimacy and understanding their opinions about your relationship.

Question: Do you believe in love?

Question: What are you scared of?

Question: If you could change anything in your past,

what would it be?

Question: Have you ever had your heart broken?

Question: How long do you need before you can trust someone?

Question: What makes you feel insecure?

Question: What mistakes have you made in your past relationship?

Question: What are your regrets?

Question: What is your definition of cheating?

Question: Have you ever lost something or someone you cared about dearly?

Conversation Idea: For day 84 - 95: There is always room for growth in a relationship. Words could be said more, actions performed regularly, and the only way to know what to do would be to assess the relationship and find out. They are similar to romantic questions, but they are specifically targeting the growth and development of the relationship. Anything else that is achieved is a bonus. These questions are guaranteed to do just that.

Question: What do you think we need to work on the most in our relationship?

Question: When we are with my family, do I make you feel like you are still my priority?

Question: How would you respond if one of us was offered a job that required a lot of traveling?

Question: What is a question you have never asked me?

Question: What do you consider your best and worst qualities?

Question: Are you friends with any of your exes?
Question: Do you want to have kids (if yes, how many)?

Question: Do you have any deal-breaker, things that would make you seriously reconsider our relationship?

Question: Where do you see us in a few years?

Question: What makes me different from the other people you have been with?

Question: Do you think confessions make a relationship stronger?

Question: What did your last relationship teach you?

Conversation Idea: The relationship that your partner has in regard to their parents is going to be important in your relationship as well. If they get along with their parents, the relationship may go smoothly. If they don't get along with their parents, it could cause some issues as you both try to navigate through this issue as well. And if they get along with their parents too much, it could cause you and your partner to fight a bit.

Question: What are your feelings towards your parents?

Conversation Idea: If you already have a pet, or your partner has a pet, then it is likely that both of you have already talked about having a pet and what it would look like in your relationship. But if you are thinking about getting a pet, and you want to know what your partner thinks about doing this, then it is time to discuss this ahead of time. it is never a good idea to just show up at home and have a new pet with you. Maybe your partner has some allergies that you don't know about, or they are not ready to take on some of the responsibilities that will come with this.

Question: What are your thoughts on having a pet?

Conversation Idea: This is a good question to ask to help you figure out how your partner would spend or save their money. Spenders and savers get into relationships all the time, and many of them can make it work. But when you have two different styles that come with money, it is sometimes going to be a challenge to figure out what works and what doesn't. And money can be a big trouble when one of you likes to really save money, and the other has no problem with spending it as fast as they can.

Question: If you received $10,000 today, what would you do with it?

Conversation Idea: This is going to be a good one when your partner is going through a day that seems particularly difficult. Or if you and your partner seem to be having some problems right at that time, you may want to bring this question up to see how you are able to help and make things better.

Question: What do you feel like you need from me right now?

Conversation Idea: This is a question that you can ask the other person and yourself. You may want to respond to it out loud while the other partner listens to what you have to say. The number one factor that will determine whether a relationship is healthy and lasting is going to be how well they can manage conflict. This is going to include how well the partner is able to listen without interrupting, how well they are willing to discuss the issues, and how well they will tolerate difference and strategizing solutions together.

Question: How is the best way for me to express my anger and conflict?

Conversation Idea: This is going to give you a better insight into what your partner really enjoys in their life.

Question: What is something that you are looking forward to the next week?

Conversation Idea: This is one to open up their thoughts on what is working in the relationship, and what might need a bit more work to help them feel happier and more content with it?

Question: Am I being the right partner to you?
Conversation Idea: It is important to stop and check in regularly to see if what you are saying and doing with your partner is positively feeding the relationship. You can see if there are any things that you can do to improve this part of your relationship.

Question: What are the ways that you most experience love or feel the love from me?

Conversation Idea: This can be a fun one to talk about your favorite books and maybe get a few laughs.

Question: If you were able to be any character from a book, which one would it be?

Conversation Idea: If your partner were able to quit work tomorrow because they got a big huge inheritance, what are some of the things that they would do with all of that new-found freedom? This is a fun one to imagine and talk about because the possibilities and the limits are all going to be long gone.

Question: What would you do with your life if money wasn't something you had to worry about?

Conversation Idea: This one can be a bit more difficult, but it forces you and your partner to think past some of the basics and into what is the most important thing for you. But it is also a very critical one, and one you will need to know at some point if you and your partner stay together.

Question: What would your last wishes be were you not be able to make a health care decision?

Conversation Idea: We have this argument about what women can and can't do and likewise for men as well. Couples often don't realize they restrict themselves based on their gender but disguise it as a personality trait. As a man or the dominant one in a relationship for same-sex, you may take charge of situations constantly over your partner.

Question: Are you restricting each other?

Conversation Idea: We need to sit down and learn exactly what our partner's love language really is. Understanding what ours is, and what theirs is, can really help to make a big difference in how well you are able to communicate with each other, and how you can show one another how you love.

Question: What do you consider is your love language?

Conversation Idea: Is there something in particular you do that puts off your partner or makes them want to make the relationship uncomfortable? If it's not on your part that you are uncomfortable or unloved enough find out if there is anything you can do to alleviate the situation. Perhaps you can bring it to your partner's notice that you haven't been feeling loved enough, or that you are uncomfortable.

Question: Is there anything I can do to feel more comfortable or loved?

Conversation Idea: People are different, and as such, will respond differently to various conditions. What if it is your actions or words that are ruining your relationship? You wouldn't know if you don't ask. Ask your partner if there is anything you have done which hurt or upset them. One practical way of tackling crises is identifying possible causal factors and nipping them in the bud. Sometimes, these actions may not necessarily be hurtful in themselves and may seem right by you, but your partner may not feel the same way. This may lead to friction in your connection, which may spark a potential crisis capable of ruining the relationship.

Question: Is there something I have done lately that has hurt or upset you unknowingly?

Conversation Idea: As much as you know your partner, you are well aware that there are certain activities he or she cherishes doing with you. Such activities may range from simple tasks like hugs and kisses and cuddles and shared meals, to complex tasks like working on projects together, vacationing together, et al. These activities are sometimes the things your partner looks forward to, because your involving them makes them feel all the most loved. It doesn't mean that you neglect loving them all the while, or that your show of love in other ways doesn't count. No. Just as variations exist in behavior, tastes differ too.

Question: Is there any activity (cuddles, hugs, kisses) in particular that would help you feel more loved?

Conversation Idea: Say your partner just experienced something tragic or emotionally tasking, you shouldn't assume what they would like from you during such times. We all need different things to process a negative experience and do so at different speeds. Your partner may not tell you that you are doing it wrong, but it is a display of insensitivity to just do what you feel is right, Instead of asking. Inquiring from them about their needs at such times doesn't mean you don't know them. It shows respect, both for the situation and your partner.

Question: In this period, do you need time alone or more closeness?

Conversation Idea: You must also be willing to listen to what they have to say without behaving defensively. Don't take anything as an affront. This type of conversation is important to the longevity of your relationship. Should they tell you they have never or no longer find sex exciting with you, try not to get hurt by this. Instead, ask them what could be done to spice things up.

Question: What do you think about our sex life?

Conversation Idea: If your partner is usually busy and stressed out, then this is a good time to be empathetic and considerate. It may not be fair to confront them about how much time they are not spending with you, or start going on about your stressful day. Be supportive and ask to know what you can do to help. That's what partnership truly is about.

Question: Is there anything I can do to alleviate your stress?

Conversation Idea: This is a question you can ask the other person and yourself. You may want to respond to it out loud while the other partner listens to what you have to say. The number one factor that will determine whether a relationship is healthy and lasting is going to be how well they can manage conflict. This is going to include how well the partner is able to listen without interrupting, how well they are willing to discuss the issues, and how well they will tolerate difference and strategizing solutions together.

Question: How is the best way for me to express my anger and conflict?

Conversation Idea: This is going to give you a better insight into what your partner really enjoys in their life.

Question: What is something that you are looking forward to the next week?

Conversation Idea: This is one to open up their thoughts on what is working in the relationship, and what might need a bit more work to help them feel happier and more content with it?

Question: Am I being the right partner to you?

Conversation Idea: Keep this one serious. Do you want to know what things, other than you, they can't live without? This gives you some insight into what things they see as important, and what things are less important.

Question: What are three things that are so important to you, that you are not able to live without?

Conversation Idea: If you were able to be any character from a book, which one would it be? This can be a fun one to talk about your favorite books and maybe get a few laughs.

Question: What are the ways that you most experience love or feel the love from me?

Conversation Idea: This is a great question that allows you to really think back on how far your life has gone since you were a teenager, and to explore some of the ways that maybe you would change things if you could.

Question: If you could go back in time to who you were as a teenager, what are the two words that you would tell yourself?

Conversation Idea: This allows your partner to really explore their imagination and what makes them the most excited overall from one day to the next. You can discuss what would happen in the day, what the weather would be like, and who would be there.

Question: Describe what the perfect day would be for you.

Conversation Idea: Don't let them delve into a lot of negativity on this one. But you do want to get a better idea of what they consider are their strengths and what they think are some of their weaknesses along the way.

Question: If you were able to change one thing about yourself, what would this be?

Conversation Idea: It is likely that you don't get a chance to follow your partner around and see what happens during their day. And no matter how close the two of you are, or how long you have been together there are probably a few things that you haven't gotten a chance to talk about when it comes to your day to day life. Asking them to walk you through a typical day can really help you to learn more about them, what they have to go through from one day to the next, and how you could make things a bit easier for them if you can.

Question: If I walked around in your day for one day, what would I experience?

Conversation Idea: If your partner were able to quit work tomorrow because they got a big huge inheritance, what are some of the things that they would do with all of that new-found freedom? This is a fun one to imagine and talk about because the possibilities and the limits are all going to be long gone.

Question: What would you do with your life if money wasn't something you had to worry about?

Conversation Idea: This is another one of those ice breakers that allows you to have some fun, and warm-up for some of the harder questions that you may need to talk about a bit. It is kind of fun to learn what your partner is going to say about their three wishes, and you both can laugh about the silly topics and ideas that you decide to bring up. Both of you should take some time to discuss what three wishes you would be interested in.

Question: If you had three wishes, what would those three wishes be?

Conversation Idea: All of us are afraid of something, even if we have never admitted it before. And you may have read that last question and realized that you have never asked your partner what their fears are, and maybe you have no idea about the answer at all. You do not want to pressure your partner and try to make them approach situations that scare them and make them anxious. But it is hard to support your partner through this if you don't know what the fear is. When you know what fear is all about, you can also ask them how you can support and help them become more comfortable with that situation.

Question: What do you think is your greatest fear?

Conversation Idea: This is one that is going to make sure that the conversation is going to end on a positive note. This allows both of you to think about something that is happy, and fun and wonderful influences in your lives.

Question: What is the best thing that you think has ever happened in your life?

Conversation Idea: Part of living a fulfilled and happy life is feeling that you are making a meaningful contribution to the world in some way. It could be through your job, raising your children well, through some outside interest or hobby you find meaningful or service-oriented, or directly in the way you live your life. Ask your partner what mark he or she wants to leave on the world after he or she dies. How do you want your children and family to remember you?

Question: What kind of legacy do we want to leave our children and the world?

Conversation Idea: You might enjoy your job, or it might be far from ideal, but if you had the option to change careers today, what would you do? What did you dream of being when you were a child? If you had all of the talent, ability, skills, and education necessary for a particular career, what would it be? Allow each other to fantasize and brainstorm about your dreams for the perfect career.

Question: If you didn't have the job you have now, what would be your dream career?

Conversation Idea: We all have hopes and dreams for things we want to accomplish, places we want to visit, and things we want to see. Both of you take a minute and write down ten items for your bucket list. Then take turns sharing what's on your list. Where is there crossover between your items? Are there bucket list items you want to share as a couple? Which items are you ready to prioritize and plan out for the near future (in the next year or two)?

Question: What are ten things on your bucket list?

Conversation Idea: This is a fun question to stimulate imagination and express your wildest dreams. Come up with a specific amount of money you might win, and talk together about how you'd want to use the money. Enjoy thinking about the freedom and opportunity you'd have with all the money you'd win. Aside from spending on your own desires, how could you use the money to help others, create something useful, or leave a legacy?

Question: If we won the lottery, what would you want to do with the money?

Conversation Idea: Do you have relationships with friends, business associates, and family that you'd like to strengthen? Are there new friendships you'd like to develop or old friends you'd like to reconnect with? Think about what you are missing in your social life and personal relationships and what you'd like to do to find more joy and depth in your various relationships. Ask how you can help your partner reach his or her goals and wishes concerning these relationships.

Question: Who would you like to spend more time with, and what relationships would you like to develop?

Conversation Idea: There are so many beautiful, interesting, exciting places to live in the world. You might live in your city because it was where you grew up, you found a job there, or maybe you moved to be with your partner. If the world was your oyster, where would you settle down? Think about your ideal lifestyle and the kinds of people and activities you enjoy. What cities best match those? Do you envision ever moving to another city?

Question: If we didn't live in this city, where would you like to live?

Conversation Idea: If going to work were optional, but you still received your paycheck, how would you spend your time? What activities would bring you fulfillment and joy? How would your lives be different? Talk together about perfect lifestyle for you as a couple if you could reclaim the hours a day you work.

Question: If you didn't have to work, how would you spend your time?

Conversation Idea: You both have had many accomplishments and achievements throughout your lives. Which of these, whether in your youth or adulthood, has made you the proudest? Why did it make you feel proud? Listen to each other tell the story of this special moment and acknowledge the accomplishment and feelings your partner shares.

Question: What do you feel most proud of?

Conversation Idea: Both of you might have personal goals you've been nurturing. Maybe you want to run a marathon, write a book, or learn to speak a language. Share your personal goals with your partner and find out how you can support each other in reaching those goals. Is there anything getting in the way of attainting your goals, and, if so, what can you both do to address these roadblocks?

Question: What do you personally want to achieve during the next five to ten years?

Conversation Idea: For some people, retirement means moving to the mountains or the beach and enjoying uninterrupted free time. For others, it might mean traveling the world or starting a non-profit. Talk about how you both envision your retirement years. Where would you live? How would you spend your time? If you differ in your vision, how can you create a retirement scenario that works for both of you?

Question: What do you see us doing during our retirement years?

Conversation Idea: By working through these

questions together, you have initiated a new level of intimacy, compassion, and understanding between you. A love relationship is a work in progress, and, like a garden, it needs constant attention and care. What are your ongoing goals for the health of your relationship? Where do you see areas that need improvement and what specific actions can you work on daily? As individuals, what do each of you need to work on related to anger, emotional reactivity, compassion, kindness, communication, honesty, confidence, trustworthiness, stress, health, reliability, or commitment?

Question: How can we continue to improve our relationship and become closer, kinder, and more intimate?

Conversation Idea: Do each of you have specific financial goals for the future? What do you want your net worth to be? Have you thought about saving for a major purchase or for your children's education? Have you put together a retirement plan? Is there debt that needs to be paid off? You might have differing financial goals, or one of you might have considered these goals and the other isn't focused on it. As a couple, you need to be on the same page about your financial goals and how you are going to reach them.

Question: What are your long-term financial goals for us?

Conversation Idea: Once you discuss your financial goals and come to an agreement on what your joint goals should be, think about the specific actions and plans you want to implement to make those goals happen. How and when will you implement them? Who will be in charge of taking the actions? Even if one of you is more active with financial planning than the other, it's important that all plans and decisions are made together. Neither of you wants to feel an "imbalance of power" when it comes to your finances.

Question: What should we do to stay on top of our financial goals?

Conversation Idea: Our personalities, families of origin, and life experiences determine our attitudes about money. Some people view it as a scarce resource and hold tightly to what they have. Others see money as always available and abundant and have few fears about spending. Some see making money as an interesting pursuit while others view it simply as a means to an end. As a couple you have an obligation to balance your values and beliefs to find common ground between you. Talk about your attitude related to money with your partner and how you developed the values and beliefs you have.

Question: What are your values and beliefs about money?

Conversation Idea: Wherever you are in your life right now, you likely have some concerns about money. Maybe you want to make more. Maybe you're concerned about your debt. It could be that you worry about the stock market and how your money is performing. Allow your partner to express his or her worries and just listen without passing judgment or reinforcing those concerns. Ask your partner if he or she wants to discuss possible ways to address the worries.

Question: What causes you the most worry or frustration about money now?

Conversation Idea: Talk together about the way you both handle money and how your habits are similar. In what areas of spending and saving do you both agree? For now, just talk about the common ground and how you are alike in this regard. Even if you have differences in how you handle money, it's important to focus on the similarities and see that you share common values and behaviors.

Question: How are our spending and saving habits complementary?

Conversation Idea: You will likely have areas of difference in your spending and saving habits. These differences might have caused conflict or resentment in the past. Without pointing fingers or getting defensive, simply articulate how you are different. Then ask your spouse more about the emotions behind his or her habits. Money habits often have emotional drivers. For example, you might ask, "How does it make you feel to put $500 in savings every month?" or "What is the deeper reason you want to buy a new car rather than a used one?" Ask these questions with the real intention of understanding the feelings behind the behaviors.

Question: How are our spending and saving habits different?

Conversation Idea: Having a better understanding of your spouse's values and emotions about money can help you manage disagreements about it. If you have defined your values as a couple and you agree on your financial goals for the future, you should be able to return to those for guidance in addressing disagreements. This requires you are both equally committed to your mutual values and goals. However, there will be exceptions and times each of you might want to stray from your goals for a new priority or opportunity. Talk about how you can address these future issues without it becoming a heated discussion involving blame or shame. Determine your hot buttons about money conflict and how you can avoid these hot buttons and have a productive conversation.

Question: How should we handle it if we have a disagreement about money?

Conversation Idea: Some people don't want any debit except their mortgage. Others are fine using credit cards, financing their car, or taking out a student loan. What are your individual attitudes about debt and how much you should carry as a couple? If you disagree about this, how can you determine an acceptable amount of debt? Once you mutually determine this, are you both committed to sticking to the agreement?

Question: What kind of debt do you feel is acceptable

for us?

Conversation Idea: Saving money is essential for reaching your financial goals and dealing with any unexpected emergencies or life priorities. If you are living beyond your means or have debt, you need to address these. But it's still important to get into the habit of putting money aside, even if it's a small amount. Based on your financial goals and your current level of debt, you should have some idea of how much you should save. This might require you to cut back on expenses or alter your lifestyle. Are you both willing to do this? Discuss together how much you believe is realistic to set aside each month.

Question: How much money should we save each month?

Conversation Idea: Every person wants to be different; "the one and only." They want to be the special one that arouses new unfamiliar feelings from their significant others, however to understand why partners act a certain way or why they have certain views and perspective of relationships, we need to take a look at past partners and previous relationships and relationships with people around them.

Question: Do past relationships and our relationship with other people influence our emotional needs and expectations?

Conversation Idea: In the same way that past partners and previous relationships can influence new relationships, behaviors and attitudes towards the new relationship, holding on to residual feelings from previous relationships also affects new relationships. These residual feelings could either be positive feelings or negative feelings towards an individual's past partner and relationship.

Question: Do we have residual feelings from previous relationships and how does it affect present relationship?

Conversation Idea: All relationships require efforts, commitment, and patience to stay alive and work. It is easy to drift apart and lose the emotional connection between them when partners get too comfortable with each other and stop trying to keep the emotional connection intact. In order for partners to stay emotional connection even when they are physically apart, there need to be a level of trust and emotional security between partners that allows them to rest easy even when they are thousands of miles away from each other.

Question: How do you keep connected and in sync with each other?

Conversation Idea: In romantic relationships, the level of emotional depth and dependency between both partners determines the strength of that relationship. Communicating with your partner does not guarantee that you do understand what he/she is going through and often, partners may feel like their significant other listens out of sense of duty, not because they genuinely care or feel the way they do which could lead to him/her feeling small and insignificant.

Question: How deep is our emotional connection?

Conversation Idea: If one's partner is not sensitive enough, they might find it difficult to express absolute emotions towards the other. They are less familiar with the act of absorbing people's emotions or physical symptoms. They filter the world through logics and facts. The trademark of an empath is feeling and absorbing other people's emotions. Displaying this attribute would require a selfless attitude and an understanding that not everyone thinks and feels the same way.

Question: Is my partner emphatic towards my feelings?

Conversation Idea: It is important for partners to have common goals and interests in a relationship. When partners share common interest, it reduces the probability of conflicts and disagreements between them and deepens their sense of closeness, intimacy an emotional connection.

Question: Do we have shared interests and goals?

Conversation Idea: There is an infinite number of causes for disagreements in relationships ranging from major reasons like incompatibility in partner's behavior, parenting methods, communication methods, finances, etc. But there are generally specific reasons why partners engage in conflicts and disagreements with each other.

Question: Why do we disagree?

Conversation Idea: Understanding the specific issues causing disagreements in relationships can be a first step towards reconciliation of conflicts and disagreements. Partners in a committed relationship have an equal partnership and have to make every decision affecting their lived together.

Question: What issues do we disagree on?

Conversation Idea: Maintaining intimacy is crucial for the success of every long term relationship. Existing intimacy between partners helps both partners to understand each other, identify unspoken feelings of hurt faster and to better empathize with each other.

Question: How do we reconnect and maintain intimacy after resolving conflict?

Question: What is the most important lesson about love that your partner has taught you?

Question: If you and your partner had to permanently move to another country, who would you both reach out to first to say goodbye? Who would you both not allow to visit?

Question: If you created an Anniversary card for your partner that required you to summarize your feelings in a sentence of 25 words or less, what would you write?

Question: What advice did your parent(s) give you about love? Do you feel that it has been applicable to your relationship? Why or why not?

Question: Describe to your partner a memory from early in your relationship that stands out to you as being significant. If you were granted the opportunity to exchange (and forget) that memory for another one equally as significant in the future, would you take it? Why or why not?

Question: Look around at the colors that surround you, those on the walls of the room you are in, those on the clothes you are wearing, those on the items of décor of the room you are sitting in. What do you think these colors say about you, your partner and your relationship?

Question: Discuss the kindest thing that you feel your partner has ever done for you. Then discuss the most selfish thing you have done to your partner.

Question: Describe your favorite weather related memory that you and your partner have shared.

Question: If you and your partner could go back and document with a video camera one day from your relationship, which day would each of you pick and why?

Question: What does your partner unconsciously do, or say, that you have always found to be sexy or attractive?

Question: If each of you was guaranteed an honest answer to three questions that you could ask the other, what three questions would you ask?

Question: What one thing about sex did you learn from a previous relationship, or from your friends when you were a teenager?

Question: If you could each send a message to your current selves from the person you were during the first year of your marriage, what would you write? How might that message change your current relationship?

Question: What is a favorite memory of a road trip that you and your partner took that is within six hours of your current home, or the home you lived in at the time your took the trip?

Question: Describe an event that you and your partner have planned together that you are looking forward to. Why is this event so special to the two of you?

Question: How did you describe your partner to a close friend, or family member, after your first date?

Question: Talk about a time in your life when you felt the most confident and secure. Would you be willing to go back to that period of time for one year, knowing that you could return to your current relationship, but without all the skills and accumulated wisdom that you acquired since that time?

Question: Think back to a time in your relationship when you both, as a couple, had to give up something you wanted for something you needed. Talk about the circumstances that lead you to that decision and how that situation ultimately brought you closer.

Question: What three words describe your current sex life?

Question: If you were to die suddenly, what would you most regret not having said to your partner?

Question: What is your favorite thing to do alone? Why do you prefer to do that activity without your partner?

Question: If you could change one thing about the way you were raised that you feel has made a negative impact on your relationship with your partner, what would it be?

Question: If you could switch one quality of your partner that you admire with one quality of your own, which of theirs would you choose? Which quality of yours would your partner want to exchange for their own?

Question: If you were given the choice of having your partner be forever either smarter or more attractive than you are at the current moment, which would you choose?

Question: You want to surprise your partner with sex in an unusual place. Describe where that place would be.

Question: What is one trait that you have acquired since you met your partner that you can attribute solely to their influence on you?

Question: What is something you and your partner can agree that you did better in the past than you can do now? Do each of you feel that this ability will get better, worse or stay the same with time?

Question: If you and your partner could watch the sunrise from anywhere in the world, where would it be?

Question: What part(s) of your body are you especially proud of? Which parts, if given the opportunity, you would have “improved”?

Question: List two goals that you and your partner never discussed, but have been created through events that have occurred throughout the course of your relationship. Now that you have identified them, will you keep them as motivators, or would you like to replace them with two different goals? If so, what are your new goals?

Question: Share with your partner a list of people with whom you have given a piece of your heart. Include past loves, best friends, family members, or anyone else who has earned a special place in your life.

Question: Talk about a time when one, or both, of you broke the rules or went against what you were told to do (or not do). What did you learn from this experience? If given the chance, would you do it again?

Question: Select a photograph from your childhood. Talk with your partner about the person you were behind the image. What does the picture not reveal about you? What were your dreams? What were your challenges? Do any still remain for you today?

Question: Talk about a time you left your family home for good. What were the circumstances – leaving for college, a new job, moving in with friends? Describe your emotions and what you left behind physically and emotionally.

Question: What are the questions of life that you don't know the answers for?

Question: Your partner is going away on a trip for two months with limited access to phone and/or email. What would you write on a note-card that you would slip into their luggage before they left?

Question: What is one article of clothing that your partner owns that you would like to throw away? Why?

Question: What motto would you both create for your relationship? Why? What symbol would you both design to signify the meaning of your motto?

Question: What fear has your partner helped you to outgrow?

Question: What topic do you feel you know more about than your partner? Do they agree? What topic do they feel they know more about than you? Do you agree?

Question: Tell your spouse the story behind one of your scars, or unusual mannerisms.

Question: You are wide awake at 3 am. What thoughts, worries and dreams are going through your head that you can share now with your partner?

Question: What five adjectives would you use to describe your partner when you first realized you loved them? Which five would you use now? Which would you use 10 years from now?

Question: What is the best gift that your partner has ever given you? What does your partner remember about buying, making or acquiring that particular gift?

Question: What skill or talent do you possess that you have never shown your partner?

Question: Your partner has just handed you a box and it's not your birthday or anniversary. Describe what you found inside it.

Question: Talk about your favorite ritual, routine or habit(s) you have as a couple, or a family. Why are these so important to you individually?

Question: Share with your partner a time when something big in your life started off as something small and seemingly insignificant.

Question: Is there a smell that when you experience it causes you to have fond memories of a person or event, or evokes a physical response in you such as a smile, a blush, a tear or a shudder? Talk to your partner about these responses and the memory them.

Question: Discuss a time in your life, either individually or as a couple, when the only comfort you had was hope. What belief did you have that sustained you and helped you to move forward?

Question: Do you help one another to have more self-esteem, or do you tend to find fault with each other? Are his/her needs as important to you as your own?

Question: How do you each treat your own parents? Do you respect them as individuals and respect their position and authority? (It is likely that you will treat each other the same way you each treat own family).

Question: Do your friends use foul language? Does your family use foul language?

Question: Do you use foul language at home? In public? With your family?

Question: Are you satisfied with the quality and quantity of friends you currently have? Would you like to be more involved socially? Are you overwhelmed socially, and do you need to cut back on such commitments?

Question: What are your partner's needs for cultivating or maintaining friendships outside of your relationship? Is it easy for you to support those needs, or do they bother you in any way?

Question: Sometimes we lose perspective and the best source for opinions is our friends and family. What does your friends and family think of him or her?

Question: Do you feel the need to maintain relationships with your past boyfriends/girlfriends? Why or why not?

Question: Would you expect him or her not to spend any time alone with friends that are of the opposite sex?

Question: Do you anticipate maintaining your single lifestyle after you are married? That is: will you spend just as much time with your friends, family and work? Why or why not?

Question: What type of relationship do you want your spouse to have with your friends?

Question: Do you love to have guests in your home for entertainment?

Question: Who are your friends? Identify at least three. What is it that makes them your friends?

Question: Do you each find yourself continually looking for appropriate ways to make the other happy? Or are you each seeking your own happiness and interests without first considering those of the other?

Question: Are you each free to be yourself when you are together, or must you always be on guard?

Question: Are there hobbies that he/she engages in that are reckless or too time-consuming? Are you spending less time with him/her because of it?

Question: If there is an issue in your relationship that could cause a divorce, what would that issue be? What spiritual ways would he/she use to overcome it?

Question: One of the most predictive traits for compatibility is if you can sense the other's sadness. Can you tell when he/she is upset?

Question: At this stage in your relationship, do you still feel the need to be "on your best behavior," or are you comfortable being yourself?

Question: What do you fear in your relationship?

Question: If there is one thing you could do but are not currently doing to make your relationship more meaningful, what is it?

Question: Do you truly enjoy each other's company? Or do you just enjoy each other when you are doing things you like to do?

Question: What do you not like about him or her? (Research tells us you can't change another person, you can only change yourself). What can you not live with, that he/she does?

Question: What do each of you bring to the relationship?

Question: Do you uplift one another in public, or do you poke fun at him or her just to get a laugh from your friends?

Question: Do you talk positively about him or her to your friends or coworkers? Or, do you dwell mostly on the negative things?

Question: Do you agree on music? Is there music that you listen to that is inappropriate? Would you allow your future children to listen to it?

Question: Does each of you inspire the other to do his/her best in studies, jobs, church callings, and other significant responsibilities? Or do you both live below your standards and ideals when you are together?

Question: Do you encourage each other's hobbies and talents?

Question: If someone were to put you down, would your significant other stand up for you or ignore the situation?

Question: Is your significant other overly jealous and possessive? Does he or she need to know exactly where you are at all times of the day? Does he or she call to check up on you?

Question: Do you get jealous easily and mistrust for no reason?

Question: Is he or she more giving than you? Are you too selfish?

Question: As you get older, does your significant other expect or want you to get plastic surgery to improve your looks? How do you feel about that? If you wanted plastic surgery, would he or she be okay with that?

Question: Do you think it is okay to divorce someone solely for being diagnosed with depression? What if you had children?

Question: Would you be opposed to mental health treatment?

Question: If you have male/female friendships and these relationships made your significant other uncomfortable, would you end them for him or her?

Question: Do you need to hide who you really are? Or are you confident that you are fully accepted and loved?

Question: What are your views on divorce? Did you come from a divorced family? Do you think it is okay to divorce when children are involved? Or would you stay married despite your feelings, for the sake of the children?

Question: What type of relationship do you want with your children? Do you expect to be their best friend and give them everything you never got? Or, do you plan to let them experience what "earning a dollar" means?

Question: Is trust automatic until something occurs that takes it away, or does it evolve over time?

Question: Are you the type of person that would discuss your private business, whether it is your sex life or relationships, with a best friend other than your current partner? How would you feel if he/she did the same?

Question: If you have children from a previous marriage, will your significant another get along with your children? Will he/she be able to handle dealing with an ex-spouse?

Question: If your past husband or wife is deceased, are

you marrying too soon? (Each person is unique.) Are you comparing your past relationship with the present too much?

Question: What is your definition of “flirting”?

Question: If one of us cheats, what is the outcome?

Question: Is there anything in your past I should be aware of?

Question: If your past boyfriends/girlfriends listed your most negative characteristics, what would they be?

Question: Have you ever been violent in past relationships?

Question: Do you keep letters or pictures from past relationships?

Question: Do your friends entice you to see other people? Why?

Question: As you were growing up, did you think more about the type of person you wanted to marry, or the type of person you wanted to be for your spouse? Why? Describe your thoughts.

Question: Are there any past addictions (gambling, internet pornography, etc.) from your past that your fiancé doesn't know about?

Question: Have you ever been able to overcome a bad habit? What was it?

Question: Would it concern you if he or she had

premarital sex long before he or she met you? What if he or she had that situation resolved by telling the bishop and going through the steps of repentance?

Question: Have you ever cheated on a past girlfriend or boyfriend? If so, what is your plan for never doing it again? Why should he or she believe you would never cheat on him or her?

Question: Why have you ended relationships in the past?

Question: Have you ever been involved in any criminal activity, been in jail or testified for anyone in court?

Question: Have you ever had a history of drugs, alcoholism or domestic violence? Is there a history of that in your family? Does he or she control you? Is he or she very jealous?

Question: Have you ever seen a psychologist? Been diagnosed with a mental disorder, anxiety or depression? Do you take medicine for a condition? What for, and how much?

Question: Has anyone ever had a reason not to trust either of you?

Question: What was your childhood like? Was your family an affectionate one?

Question: Have you had premarital sex and how often? Have you repented? Is being married in the temple important to you?

Question: Is there anyone in your family who is dangerous or sexually abusive?

Question: Which childhood or church experiences

influence your behavior and attitudes the most?

Question: Could any feelings of affection and romance be revived if you met a previous boyfriend or girlfriend, even though you feel strongly committed to your significant other?

Question: How is your relationship different from or similar to the ones you have had in the past?

Question: Do you have any health problems he or she should know about?

Question: Have you been married before?

Question: What would you do if you felt that you had been abused?

Question: Whom would you call for assistance, if you were being abused?

Question: Are you willing to take a physical exam before marriage?

Question: Is there an embarrassing situation in your life you don't want anyone to know about?

Question: Do you have unresolved issues in your life that you need to see the bishop or a psychologist about?

Question: If you were previously married, what part of that relationship did you contribute to the divorce? What could you have done differently to make the marriage work?

Question: Do you have enemies or anyone in your life

that would like to harm you or your future family, either financially or physically?

Question: Do you have a violent past or difficulty controlling your anger?

Question: Do you think hitting or shoving a person is okay when you're angry?

Question: Is there a secret that you are withholding from your friends or family?

Question: Does your significant other have a history of any of the following: abusing narcotics or prescription drugs, violence, jealousy, alcoholism, smoking? Do you feel they may still have this problem, or could potentially have this problem in the future?

Question: Looking back at your past relationships,

what stands out to you as the most common mistake you have made in each of them?

Question: What was the best moment in your life?

Question: What was the worst moment in your life?

Question: What is your philosophy in life?

Question: What would you like to change in yourself, why?

Question: Are you religious, what do you believe in?

Question: Do you like spending time with other people?

Question: Which parent are you closer to and why?

Question: Do you do what you always wanted to do in your life?

Question: What makes you feel satisfaction?

Question: What is your favorite book/movie of all time and why?

Question: What did you lack in important relationships for you?

Question: Mind or beauty?

Question: Have anybody ever cheated you?

Question: How would you feel when sharing a very personal, life space with a partner?

Question: What do you think when a person is ready for marriage?

Question: How do you think what parent you will be or what kind of person you would like to be?

Question: What would you do if your parents did not like your partner?

Question: Who is the only person with whom you can talk lightly about “anything”?

Question: Is there a place for your partners in your life?

Question: Have you ever lost a loved one?

Question: If you are in a bad mood, do you prefer to be alone or do you like when someone cheers you up?

Question: What is your perfect weekend?

Question: What do you think about the best friends of the opposite sex, possible?

Question: Have you ever written a diary?

Question: For what are you most grateful in your life?

Question: Do you believe in a second chance?

Question: What do your dream holidays look like?

Question: What's the craziest thing you've ever done?

Question: What do you think others do not understand about you?

Question: You caught the "gold fish," what are your 3 wishes?

Question: Do you often think about it when you are alone?

Question: Do you like being praised?

Question: Is there something you dreamed about for a long time? Why did not you do it?

Question: What would you change in your life?

Question: What is your greatest achievement?

Question: What are you afraid of?

Question: What is the most embarrassing moment in your life?

Question: Have you ever been betrayed by a loved one?

Question: Have you forgiven people who have hurt you?

Question: What is love for you?

Question: What should your closest person know about you?

Question: When do you need loneliness?

Question: Are there topics that you don't want to talk to anyone?

Question: If you could change one thing about yourself, what would it be?

Question: Do you think "Younger You" would be happy with what you have become?

Question: How do you describe me to other people?

Question: Is there anything sexually we haven't tried

that you'd like to?

Question: Thoughts on sexual toys?

Question: What do you think is the biggest problem in the world today?

Question: If I asked you to cook me dinner, what would you make me?

Question: Do you think there is a difference between having sex and making love? What is it?

Question: How do you think aging will affect your attraction to me?

Question: What do I need to know about your past sex

life?

Question: Have you ever had your heart broken? What happened?

Question: Have you ever stolen anything before?

Question: What movie are you embarrassed to admit you love?

Question: What was the first movie we saw together?

Question: What is one thing people get wrong about you?

Question: What do you wish people would know about you?

Question: How do you feel about lying in general?

Question: Would you lie to protect somebody from a painful truth?

Question: What would you want to change about me?

Question: IF money did not matter, what would you do with your time?

Question: What would you do if someone says something bad about me?

Question: What is your best memory of our first kiss?

Question: What is the most romantic thing I've ever done for you?

Question: What makes you the happiest about our relationship?

Question: What song reminds you of me?

Question: Which is my favorite band of all times?

Question: Do you find it easy or hard to love yourself?

Question: If you could spend one day in someone else's shoes, who would it be?

Question: What is the most daring thing you've done so far?

Question: If a genie gave you three wishes, what would they be?

Question: If you had just one day to live, what would you do?

Question: Which animal do you think I represent the most? And why?

Question: In a score from 1-10, which one represents my kissing skills? What needs improvement?

Question: Is there any time you have felt disrespected in our relationship?

Question: What is the worst part about us fighting?

Question: How we can improve the way we argue and/or disagree?

Conclusion

Thanks for making it through to the end of "365 connecting questions for couples," let's hope it was informative and able to provide you with all of the tools you need to achieve your goals whatever they may be.

The next step is to set up some time for you and your partner to sit down, in a neutral spot where you are both comfortable and ready to be open, and discuss some of the topics and questions that are brought up in this guidebook. There are a lot of different topics that we brought up in here, and while some of them are going to be easy and can even make you laugh as you learn more about one another, some are going to be tough, and may take a bit more time and effort to get through.

The important thing to remember here is that you need to be open and willing to discuss these topics with one another, and you need to be willing to actually get through them. There is no rush here, and if you need to sit down a few different times to just get through one of the topics, that is fine. This is your relationship and the only way that it is going to work the way that you would like.

These questions are meant to open you and your partner up to one another. They are meant to bring the two of you together. Taking your time, being open and honest with one another, and letting these questions bring you together, rather than making you angry, will bring your relationship to a brand-new level. When you are ready to see this happen, make sure to check out this guidebook to help you get started.

It is highly encouraging to read my two previous books: **"How to be an adult in relationships"** and **"Relationship therapy workbook"** to learn more about relationship communication.

Made in the USA
Monee, IL
17 November 2021

82333322R00066